# Oboe Solos

*with Piano Accompaniment*
*Arranged and Edited by Jay Arnold*

Order No. AM 40387
International Standard Book Number: 0.8256.2099.6

*Exclusive Distributors:*
Music Sales Corporation
257 Park Avenue South, New York, NY 10010 USA
Music Sales Limited
8/9 Frith Street, London W1V 5TZ England
Music Sales Pty. Limited
120 Rothschild Street, Rosebery, Sydney NSW 2018 Australia

Printed in the United States of America by
Vicks Lithograph and Printing Corporation

# Contents

| | Piano | Instrument |
|---|---|---|
| BOURREE . . . . . . . . . . . . . . . . . . . . . . . . . . . . . . . . . . . . . . Georg Friedrich Handel | 10 | 119 |
| CANTABILE . . . . . . . . . . . . . . . . . . . . . . . . . . . . . . . Pietro Locatelli | 8 | 118 |
| CARNATION (Concert Valse) . . . . . . . . . . . . . . . . . . . . . . . . . . Bruno Labate | 66 | 146 |
| CHANT SANS PAROLES, Op. 40, No.6 . . . . . . . . . . . . . . . Peter I. Tschaikowsky | 32 | 130 |
| CONCERTO IN F MINOR . . . . . . . . . . . . . . . . . . . . . . . . Georg Philipp Telemann | 102 | 156 |
| EASTERN ROMANCE . . . . . . . . . . . . . . . . . . . . . . . . . N. Rimsky-Korsakoff | 18 | 123 |
| EINSAME BLUMEN, Op. 82, No. 3 (Lonely Flowers) . . . . . . . . . . . . . Robert Schumann | 26 | 127 |
| GAVOTTE . . . . . . . . . . . . . . . . . . . . . . . . . . . . Johann Sebastian Bach | 4 | 116 |
| INDIAN CANZONETTA, Op. 100, No. 2 . . . . . . . . . . . . . . . . . . . . Anton Dvorak | 28 | 128 |
| LA CINQUANTAINE . . . . . . . . . . . . . . . . . . . . . . . . . . . . Gabriel-Marie | 16 | 122 |
| LEGENDE PASTORALE, Op. 138 (From "Scotch Scenes") . . . . . . . Benjamin Godard | 44 | 136 |
| MINUET . . . . . . . . . . . . . . . . . . . . . . . . . . . . . . . . Nicholas Amani | 14 | 121 |
| ON WINGS OF SONG . . . . . . . . . . . . . . . . . . . . . . . . Felix Mendelssohn | 24 | 126 |
| ORIENTALE, Op. 50 (The Kaleidoscope) . . . . . . . . . . . . . . . . . . . . Cesar Cui | 22 | 125 |
| RIGAUDON . . . . . . . . . . . . . . . . . . . . . . . . . . Jean-Philippe Rameau | 12 | 120 |
| ROMANCE NO. 1, Op. 94 . . . . . . . . . . . . . . . . . . . . . . . Robert Schumann | 70 | 147 |
| ROMANCE NO. 2, Op. 94 . . . . . . . . . . . . . . . . . . . . . . . Robert Schumann | 74 | 148 |
| ROMANCE NO. 3, Op. 94 . . . . . . . . . . . . . . . . . . . . . . . Robert Schumann | 79 | 149 |
| SARABANDE . . . . . . . . . . . . . . . . . . . . . . . . . . . . Arcangelo Corelli | 6 | 117 |
| SLAVONIC DANCE, Op. 72, No. 2 . . . . . . . . . . . . . . . . . . . . . Anton Dvorak | 36 | 132 |
| SOLVEJG'S SONG . . . . . . . . . . . . . . . . . . . . . . . . . . . . Edvard Grieg | 20 | 124 |
| SONATA NO. 1 . . . . . . . . . . . . . . . . . . . . . . . . . Georg Friedrich Handel | 50 | 138 |
| SONATA NO. 2 . . . . . . . . . . . . . . . . . . . . . . . . . Georg Friedrich Handel | 55 | 140 |
| SONATA NO. 3 . . . . . . . . . . . . . . . . . . . . . . . . . Georg Friedrich Handel | 60 | 143 |
| SONATA, K. V. 370 . . . . . . . . . . . . . . . . . . . . . . . Wolfgang Amadeus Mozart | 84 | 150 |
| ZEPHYRS . . . . . . . . . . . . . . . . . . . . . . . . . . . . . . . . Bruno Labate | 40 | 134 |

# Gavotte

Johann Sebastian Bach

**Allegro moderato**

**Trio**
**Scherzando**

# Sarabande

Arcangelo Corelli

**Larghetto**

# Cantabile

Pietro Locatelli

# Bourrée

G. F. Händel

**Allegretto**

# Rigaudon

**Allegretto**

Jean-Philippe Rameau

# Minuet

Nicholas Amani

# La Cinquantaine

**Andantino**

Gabriel - Marie

# Eastern Romance

N. Rimsky-Korsakoff

# Solvejg's Song

Edvard Grieg

# Orientale
## (The Kaleidoscope)

Cesar Cui, Op. 50

# On Wings Of Song

Felix Mendelssohn

# Einsame Blumen
## (Lonely Flowers)

Robert Schumann
Op. 28, No. 3

1249-23

# Indian Canzonetta

Anton Dvorak
Op. 100, No. 2

**Poco più mosso**

**Meno mosso, Tempo I**

# Chant Sans Paroles

P. I. Tschaikowsky
Op. 40, No. 6

**Allegro moderato**

# Slavonic Dance

Anton Dvorak
Op. 72, No. 2

# Zephyrs

Bruno Labate

# Légende Pastorale
## (From "Scotch Scenes")

Benjamin Godard, Op. 138

**Andante quasi adagio**

# Sonata No. 1

G. F. Händel

# Sonata No. 2

G. F. Händel

**Allegro**

58

# Sonata No. 3

G. F. Händel

**Allegro**

# Carnation

## Concert Valse

Bruno Labate

Coda

# Romance No. 1

Robert Schumann, Op. 94

# Romance No. 2

Robert Schumann,
Op. 94

Poco piu vivo

75

# Romance No. 3

Robert Schumann, Op. 94

Coda

# Sonata

W. A. Mozart, K. V. 370

# Rondo

# Concerto In F Minor
## I

Georg Philipp Telemann

# II

**Largo ma non troppo**

# III